Stands Alone, Faces, and Other Poems

Stands Alone, Faces, and Other Poems

by
Patrick Russell LeBeau

Michigan State University Press
East Lansing

∞ The paper used in this publication meets the
minimum requirements of ANSI/NISO Z39.48–1992 (R 1997)
(Permanence of Paper).

Michigan State University Press
East Lansing, Michigan 48823-5202

04 03 02 01 00 99   1 2 3 4 5 6 7 8 9

Library of Congress Cataloging-in-Publication Data
   LeBeau, Patrick Russell, 1958-
      Stands alone, Faces, and other poems / by Patrick Russell
   LeBeau.
      p. cm.

ISBN 0-87013-533-3 (alk. paper)
1. Indians of North America — Poetry. I. Title.
PS3562.E2632 S73 1999
811'.54 — dc21
                              99-6504
                              CIP

Book and cover design by Nicolette Rose

Visit Michigan State University Press on the World-Wide Web at:
www.msu.edu/unit/msupress

CONTENTS

Stands Alone

referring to the man known as ...

HUNTER

DEER DRAGGER

Browser—
Buck Rubs—
Your Presence is evident.
I wait for your return.
As Deerslayer
Food Provider fall.

Red hoof prints—
Bloody snow
Food Provider fall
Animal strength die,
You give for your death.

Pollen, tobacco to feed
The spirit—
Food Provider fall.
Long range, short range—
Blind behind the branches—
Give that animal his death

He staggers.
He falls,
Blood clots—lung shot,
Whispering, whistling, wheezing song of buck.
Provider for the two legged,
Steam rises as buck melts
his place in snow.

Food Provider fall,
The will of your deer nation
Is the strength that drives the rut.
I hunger and I am cold.
Provide me deer nation,
Food Provider fall.

I feel your warmth,
The steam envelopes me and
I feel your spirit,
Feed my animal strength.

I seen you jump
Into your death,
Well-placed projectile that
Ended your
Acrobatic grace.

I kissed your wet
Warm nose and thanked
You for your life.
It is the perfect gift,
Life provider.

Ambushed and killed,
Twilight hour
My patience.
Your sexual drive —
made a perfect copulation
Of life and death.

I kissed your tongue
And covered your eyes.
I tied a wreath of sage and

Sweet grass around
Your neck.

I wept for the love
Of your life.
And I enjoyed the
Moment of your death.

I cried for you.
Food Provider and
Rejoiced in your wealth.

I waited,
The spirit left,
Tobacco —
Steam dissipating.

Your covered eyes —
So I cannot notice
The black cold look of your death —
I know that you will live again.

Inside of me.
I look for you later —
Mountain descent, young pine,
Dusk, smoky haze —
Time to go.

I lift you up
Strain on my back.
We leave your home and
I drag you toward mine.

GROUSE SENT ME HOME

Seeking the mule deer,
I found a grouse
Paw prints, hoof holes,
of dog and deer
Crumpled, eyeless,
Lying still

—within a crevice—

Created by dog,
Stepped on by deer

Both I will be able to eat,
If old ground bird died from fear

—frightened by dog—

—trampled by deer—

—create this hunt—

You are sign
Dog and deer
Work
Side by side

So that when I approach,
One will bark

The other will leap
Both will escape
my
Attempt to ...

Or, deer is seeking revenge
For a ravaged brother,
Torn by canines,
Chewed and dragged
A strange thought for a deer

You are victim
And cannot tell
Only hunger
Starving for flesh,
I talk to you,
Dead on their trail

I seek this deer
Now, also this dog
What are you grouse?
A decaying,
Benevolent provider?

Kick, kick, I will kick
Dirt over you
Grouse

So I can follow this food trail,
Leaving my print,
I join dog and deer,
Unable to stop this hunt
And wanting at least one more meal

I shoulder my rifle
Pick up my pack,
Head for home, just one more
Home cooked meal

FEAR OF BEARS

He reminded me of bear, smelling
Thoughts had to be hung high in trees
Or buried deep in ground,
To preserve or discard them,
Like spent provisions or perishable
Food—but like bear,
He would try for them anyway.

Foul smelling thoughts,
Rotting like used soup cans,
Empty sardine tins, and bacon grease
You could not even go to bed with food
Smell on your clothes for fear of
Bear investigating and tasting the smell,
That is feast to his thoughts.

He has a keen nose
—that man—
I will not tell him I like his land
Suitable only for bears
That I do not fear the high climb to his
Cold Water Creek,

A nice place to fish for both man and bear,
That I am not lazy
Will wash my clothes before sleeping,
Bury my waste and hang my food
High in trees.

Bear is a foul smelling beast
His presence is known long before he is seen
The same for me with that Old Man: We smell each other:
His bear-like reek and my bacon-greased, tin can smell.

He reads my thoughts by the food I have eaten:
    Sardines: Cold mountain stream, beer and whiskey
    Bacon: Cedar trees, mountain goat, soft women,
        rough-skinned women
    Chicken Soup: Sore feet, tired legs, blistered hands
        and next week's pay.

He smells of Bear
It tells me
He is dangerous but kind
He will not hurt me
Yet, I fear and smell his powerful
Breath blowing at me.

I could eat a bear
I know that he can eat me
I stay, as breather, and to
Recognize the smell of bears
From the smell of me.

I am afraid to be mauled,
Carried away
Buried in a shallow food ditch
I should be the one to eat him,
If my fear is as great as his,
If I was as hungry inside of me.

But, I am not hungry
We do not wish to kill each other, Old

Bear, he is teaching me to survive
I should thank him, Old
Man, your kink of smell is disappearing and
Mine permeating.

These thoughts,
I hide,
High in trees, buried in ground,
Unable to speak them,
Although you are able to smell and identify them
Without being able to reach,
Strange gift? No reason to hide?
A camper's trick to do so? It is for survival.

You are a simple survivor,
Old Man,
Teaching me to fish, like bear,
To be clumsy, and safe, like bear.
Truly an experience, such confidence to be alone,
Not really frightened,
Taking and smelling
The garbage of hikers, skiers, and mountain climbers
Scaring them away and eating their garbage.
A long way back down
I wish to stay, like you man, like bear,
but,
I will never smell as you do;
I will return back down to eat
My usual breakfast, and dinner,
Only thinking, harboring thoughts,
Like a frightened camper,
Of this climb,
Only to be found
High in trees and buried deep in ground.

KNOWN AS ... **VETERAN**

HIT WITH A SLEDGE HAMMER
(Grandpa Talks About Vietnam)

He died for a good cause.
He did die literally machine-gunned down,
An act of combat.
Bullets,
"The pioneers of civilization," Buffalo Bill said,
Meant more than just cold, piercing lead.

They hit him
Like a sledge hammer
Crushing his chest.

He also lived.
What he lived for caused him
To not mind dying.
The trees, the grass, the ground, and the star nations,
Made him not mind.

The jungle reminded him of his life,
The cold, jagged earth rock of badlands
The dark pine smell of
Turtle back shaped hills, and
He would ride the pole fence line.

He decomposed rapidly
In tropical jungle,
Medi vac was late,
Jimi Hendrix was on the news.

It did not last long.
He began life
When snowflakes were falling.

He fought well.
He called himself
The free–doe–ban–dee–toe
(a Mexican-like Corn Chip Bandit)
Because,
He wore machine-gun ammo belts
Cross wise over each Shoulder,
Like Miss America girls do.

America,
They all called it the world, grandpa said
Miss America reminded him of it.

He never made it back.
He died bleeding in jungle
He saw
The big sky, night lit by star nations
Day lit by sun,
Soft green earth floor,
Different parts of his
Mother's body.
The same to him:
Jungle–Home

THE HAMMERHEADS

The Hammerheads stood
In a tight group on the eastern hill,
Standing straight up with pride,
The sun glaring around their dark solemn shapes.
Their heads nodding up and down
As if driving their pride into the ground.
They could pound your fragile body
Into a pulp of bloody flesh and broken bone
If you did not respect their strength.

The Hammerheads feed off the earth,
Rip the hair off her body,
Then turn their heads upward
With the hair, flesh and blood dangling
From the sides of their drooling mouths.
Then, with slow methodical chewing,
They devour their sustenance
Food to keep their mammoth bodies alive.

*He survived Berlin, Seoul, and Dai Nang to be smashed by one
swing of a Hammerhead. I found him, bloated body, his thick
sticky blood already soaked into the red clay. His bones
snapped and twisted, leaving his body with no defined shape,
resembling jelly—a blob of flesh. It could have been a bomb in
Berlin, Seoul, or Dai Nang. It was a Hammerhead instead.*

The Hammerheads grazed on the hill
Until the sun rose high above their heads.

Their deep lungs filling with the cold crisp air.
Their noses exhaling hot streams of steam
Turning their heads into smoking furnaces.
Their eyes red with fire and a wildness unrestrained.
Their legs long and muscular with circular knots at the
joints.

The Hammerheads stood,
Then began to move, slowly, down the hill
Into the tall grass which fell before them,
Like soldiers being cut down
By sustained machine-gun fire,
Then trampled into the womb of their mother
By Hammerheads.
Paths formed and traced back up toward
the light on top of the hill.
They stopped, submerged in the tall grass, as if forgetting
something,
Then moved more rapidly and carelessly toward the river
And the water they thirsted for.

*He had tamed a Hammerhead, the one called "Breath." He had
worked and played with him—castrated Breath who would
never learn love, only work and play. One day they both walked
toward the hill; he leading Breath. A music snake lay, hugging
the earth, blocking the path. Its song frightened Breath and
Breath jumped high and trampled him, like the grass, into the
womb of his mother.*

The Hammerheads approached the river
Some of them took walking craps at the edge
Before bowing their heads to drink.

They drank the cold water until their bellies were bloated
And they could hardly walk.
Their heads rose and looked across the river.
On the other side, some dogs refreshed themselves.
The dogs were skinny and did not drink as much.

The Hammerheads stood in a tight group on the eastern
shore,
Watching dogs, nodding their heads, their bellies full,
Watching the sun glare around shaggy, skinny shapes of
dogs,
Until the horizon burned red and slowly grew dark.

KNOWN AS ... **OLD MAN**

OLD MAN RAIN–IN–THE–FACE DRIVES A PICKUP TRUCK AROUND THE NATION AND HE REFUSES TO GIVE UP SMOKING

Coughing, choking, coughing,
cigarettes hang and dwindle
from distorted lips, elongated ears, tied to ribbon,
hanging from hair.

Clicking, kicking, clicking,
cowboy boots sticking,
gas pedals and braking,
saddle bags flapping
canteen full of whiskey.

He handled chickens and slapped hungry cows,
pissed on the hay and chipped at the ice
but now he is traveling around the nation
with the whiskey breath and cigarette lunch.

With the long drives near Turtle Mountains,
to Crazy Mountain and Uncle Long Daddy Mountain,
to bright red pocket canyons, to "Deadwood Rodeo,"
riding bare ass—Brahmin Bull—rodeo clown
Dry Gulch Whiskey.

whoring in Deadwood
whoring in Deadwood, whoring in Deadwood

Once in Topeka and once again in Portland
white-breasted women wanted to braid his hair,

play at his ears, bead his vest, yet, whiskey breath went ...
puking, puking, puking,
possibly an unexpected white woman pickup,
his prairie friend said, "shit, shit, shit,
we could've had some white ... shit, shit, shit"
            —lights a cigarette—

Eating grass on the Bighorn,
eating bass on the Bay Mill,
reading signs in Banff and eating cactus near Window
Rock,
Burning maps on Mackinac.

Burning bars on Franklin street,
running guns to Coyote Dog Soldier camp,
and burning tires on the way to Washington
and learning French in Quebec.

Breaking down near Rapid City,
getting jailed in Sioux City,
losing a wheel near Porcupine,
coughing up blood on Smoky Mountain,
and breaking an axle on Grand Teton.

Transporting one–hundred–two children
to the nation's survival school
and taking his mother to Mobile for an ear infection.

            And doing all of this to stop smoking.

Yellow Dog and Chainsaw

Dog,   you should not have pissed on the chainsaw
leaning so fortuitously on the stacked cut timber.

               stained snow freezing yellow,
               the man is too
               old for an axe

Dog,   you better hope your piss is frozen when the man
returns from drinking coffee and shoveling ash
from the fireplace.

               freezing piss coating
               the workings of the saw
               blade, nuts and bolts,
               the man can't find his axe

Dog,   you better get the hell out of here—the man wants
to boil you but first wants to shoot you in the
throat.

               angry bead is lowered
               the yellow dog is
               barking
               until he puked

Dog,   you should not have pissed on the chainsaw with
so many trees around.

               the hiss and buzzing of
               chainsaws echo in the
               wood as the man lay
               dreaming dog skeletons
               dancing on chainsaws and
               pissing on the wood

The Killing of the Yellow Dog

He stands, feet sinking in mud.
His fingers touching gently the hill that surrounds him.
His red cataract-filled eyes are unable to mold reflections
of tears, of cattle, of home, or of me holding the reins of a
horse.

The wrinkled touch of his fingers
wraps the brown star quilt around
his stoic, rigid stance.

He is content with the warmth generated
by the wind like movements of arms
beating at his side.

He is searching for the shiny guitar
lying face down beside him
with the fingers he finds it
and he attempts to play.

Old man, I have found you knee-high in the prairie grass,
coughing, trying to play that shiny guitar, bought with the
alcohol spinning, bought with the cold weather money.

You ran over the yellow dog when you brought that
instrument home.

I can forgive you for killing my dog when I see you on the
hill, unable to play songs, afraid to gnaw at the sweet air,

moving your arms frantically, you are a blur against the
white of the sky.

He stands
the mud sucking at his feet, attempting to play steel
strings that reflect brilliant shafts of yellow gumbo—the
thick mud that is always caked on the tires of his white
Ford pickup truck.

He tries to pluck out a song, when the image of the pick-
up, sliding and rolling in the mud, enters my mind—the
dog was coated with the thick gumbo and was buried
wheel well deep.

Man you are a willow and a cactus—face reflected in
steel—being absorbed by gumbo—I must have dreamed
this was so.

    Your yellow work boots
    trample grass in time
    while the fingers work
    steel of guitar strings

The music whines and whimpers
begging for talent
or at least the intricate workings of bones
resulting in the howling of familiar folk songs.

    He plays unable
    to brand eyes with
    browns of cattle
    yellows of hills
    whites of sky

Old you stand on a gumbo hill
ragged, and gnarled and loose cedar bark
the human touch causes great ruptures
and splintering

Old and tall tree
with barbed wire wrapped around the trunk
reflecting the work of fingers

A thorned life saver
embedded deep
the line is taut
vibrating the song of yellow-coated wheels
—sliding in the gumbo—

I mourn the death of my dog
as the roots and branches
touch gently the memory
of the man, stout and rigid,

now soft as clay

KNOWN AS ... **BOOTLEGGER**

WHISKEY AND A TATTOO

Spirit,
Spirit drink
Tattooed on his breath

That is not spirit
That is death

Spirit comes

Lie down man,
Lie down,
blow your tattoo on the sun

Lie down man,
Lie down,
Using your fingers touch your tongue

Spirit comes

The tattoo is you
Burning, burning
Finger, fingers

The tattoo is you
Learning, Learning
Tongue, tongues

Spirit,
Spirit drink
Tattooed on his breath

That is not whiskey
That is death.

Having Macabre Drinks of Pleasure

He has eyes like moles
He has to squint very hard to see beauty in this world
Yes, he sits in a hole of his own making
A bar stool uplifts him
His left arm dangles, then searches pockets,
Shirt pockets, then dangles, then reaches

Many would prefer him to leave
Or would think him a fragile buffalo leaf
Or an alcoholic buffoon

His eyes, my man, his eyes
Squint, like a ground hog
His cheeks puff out

He might be drunk —
The right hand speaks with signals
The juke box he is paying, the hamburger clutched by two
Hands rudely and the way he scratches and
Twists the glass that contains his drink

Many drinks —
Some drinks squat in glasses
He sees the liquid as having a brown sheep skin color
The kind he used to tan

Some drinks are moat waters of a towered castle
The watch tower liquid resembles the texture of the
tree bark

He knows back home—the stuff he made those great
canoes out of—he'd tame those water snakes with one
stroke of the carved paddle

Some drinks are lily ponds raised in
Cracked in two duck eggs
Extended on a rod made out of that translucent substance
The liquid is cool and crisp
Clear as the turquoise lakes of the Canadian Rockies

He pulls frogs and rounded flat metal from shirt pockets
Yes, he pays for the rich colored kind

He prefers to sit alone—alone—
The smell is rank
She would believe his clothes smell of
Cigarette smoke

He swivels, occasionally,
Squinting outward, sometimes he sees
Splashes of exotic people
Splotches of hued clothing
Waves of people in circuitous movement

Usually by this time, he falls asleep
Or it seems that way
When he lightly rocks, side by side
Nudging the people around him
He feels the epidermal fabric of

Her world
He sinks and presses against that exterior
He seeks warmth, death and the feel of the
Hot resilient skin of earth

Resiliency
The vision of his meditation
That one he induced in a crevice of his own making
Sweating, hungry, and wanting

He perceived objects—
Events with no existence
In his bar room reality
He wanted to see drinks existing in glasses (Manet,
Renoir)
                                    patches of paint

Anthropological exhibits
Of bar room mind—
Beer bottles, like chewed fingernails, ripped
From clutched fingers

He must face glasses alone
His skeletal mask spits
He licks dirt off skin

Provide him,
The drinks of the creek
He loves to eat the filth of the world
It's like trying to get rid of it

He squints and burrows through crowd
In the toilet he must discharge resiliency of
Mind and returns to drink—more—
Resiliency—Catholic Holy Water—Macabre drinks

The bar stays open all night, if you will,
Call it a blind pig, for no reason,
His eyes, my man, his eyes
Squint very hard to see beauty
Yes, the hole is warm and dark

                    it stinks
                    and it is dead.

Earth Trapped

He lay, prone—face in ice.
Dead, bloated, half submerged
Icy water.

He lay, alcohol spinning in his head.

Alcohol refusing to freeze his blood.

It flowed, circulated a dizzy perception.

White snow fell, pressing on his back, a burden driving
him down,
Making him stumble, slip into the ditch,
Horse hoof prints on his back, making him change,
Submerged in icy water.

He lay, thinking, his face freezing, his skin freezing,
But his mind thought—alcohol refused to let it sleep.

He lay, thinking.
He lay, knowing, occupied a space between two worlds—
a hole, a Ditch.

To the east,
a road—flattop—blacktop—whitelines—plowed snow,
snow dirty with soot, exhaust
Turning it gray.

Snow pressed on him, blanketed, smothering white—ice,
water underneath—freezing, binding him to the ground—
earth womb—
Ditch.

He thought about that road that bit of technology, confus-
ing his Perception—walking, riding, crawling, he traveled
that road.

He lay—roadside bars and rest areas—to ease his mind,
to give Him a glimpse of what was and what is.

A road, metaphor for life—a journey—
But this one is made of tar, rock, bituminous material—
Coal—
The guts of his mother!

He cried frozen tears when he thought of this.

To succeed, to overcome, to demonstrate—he had to press
those Guts into a sticky form and surface that road he
walked on.

He stumbled.
He fell.
He slipped off his horse into the ditch.
He had fallen off that road.

He remembered neon—roadside cafe—red neon shaped
into the Word bar. He remembered the road; his glasses
broken.
His face featureless without them, that bit of technology
to give him style.

Alcohol kept him alive.
His perception blurred.
He was frozen to the earth.
Face downward he thought.

He was merged—to the west a field—plowed—the soil churned—The reddish brown pigments facing the sun.

BONANZA—furrow after furrow—he puked, all that rotted Vegetation, all that bloody land came heaving out of him, until he Squirmed with dry heaves and nothing more would come.

Blood was the land he lay.
Blood was the land he perceived.
Blood was the air he breathed.
Bloody was the world he cared to feel as he looked and his guts Turned inside out.

He lay, steamroller pressing another road over his back.
Mammoth power lines hammered into his face.
Alcohol refusing to let him die.

Powdery snow fell, icy water filled the ditch.
He remained prone—refusing to let his mind freeze—
Wanting to understand
More

EARTH DEATH

somebody spoke
he heard his name
somebody spoke
he heard his name

existing, he spoke
existing, he spoke
dancing, dancing he

heard his words

"not the earth"
"not the earth"
he dreamed of the sky

"not the earth"
"not the earth"
he dreamed of dying in the sky

somebody spoke
he pulled at his ears
somebody spoke
he tried pulling off his ears

not beneath this earth
not beneath this earth
or beneath the surface of the sky

"please bury me in the sky"
"please bury me in the sky"

the ground is cold, colder than the sky
somebody spoke, he heard his name,
he heard his name

"not the cold, only the sky"
"not the cold, only the sky"

somebody spoke
he refused to hear
somebody spoke,
he refused to hear

"not the cold, give me the sky"
"not the cold, give me the sky"

somebody spoke
existing he spoke
"please, please bury me in the sky"

dancing on the surface, he jumped into the sky
dancing on the surface, he jumped into the sky

jumping, jumping, he slowly died

WHAT'S TO BE DONE WITH THESE TWO FACES

The following is true as far as it goes. I remember Grandpa Allard—my mother's Mother's father—used to tell many stories and such when we would come visiting but only if us kids would sit quietly and tend to his needs. I always brought him a pack of Camels; a brand he said he began smoking in 1917. In 1976, when I was eighteen, he told me a more serious story because he overheard my father and me discussing what I should do with my life. My father wanted me to go to college rather than throwing block in Minnesota or raising horses for the rodeo with my uncle in South Dakota. The story Grandpa Allard told was analogous both to his life and to my father's life. But, I wonder how much the story was meant for me.

As the story goes, in his youth, Grandpa Allard was a self proclaimed Frenchman from Montreal who had blue eyes. He married my mother's mother's mother. She was either full blood Chippewa or full blood Cree or simply full blood Indian of some sort; nobody knows for sure which. They all spoke Chippewa, Mitchif, French, and English. At that time, Grandpa Allard was known as the "White–Man–From–Bellcourt," who, as my mom would say, "bought all the booze for those drinking Indians." Grandpa Allard was prosperous with a very productive farm where he raised corn and sold the timber off it. He took care of my mother's family and several other families as well. Then it became known that Grandpa Allard wasn't full French and was more than half—or whatever—Cree or Chippewa. Because of this fact, as the story goes—and I am not sure how—Grandpa Allard lost his land and had to move onto the reservation with my mom's mother's family. He consequently had to admit he was "Indian" and in fact, had to be Indian for the rest of his life. At least this is what my mother, my aunts, and my uncles from Turtle Mountain tell me is true. This is the story as I remember it, doctored up with my "college education" and because of my fuzzy memory.

(Grandpa, I have brought you some tobacco so that you may tell me a story. And I have brought along a lap–top computer: this, here, electronic device I've brought from the university. I want to write all we say and gesture 'down' so that our meeting will be recorded and shared beyond ourselves.)

(All right grandson, I will accept your tobacco, and I'll accept your electronic device as well. I do this because it is winter and the story will relate to you. It will relate to you young men and women who chose to listen to the university and chose to listen to old men, old Indian men—who like the university—have many stories to tell. This, I hope, will not embarrass you, but I only wish to make our sharing worthwhile.)

(A short pause, as he lights a cigarette and drinks some water sweetened with maple syrup.)

There was this man with two friends. This man was a bit dull because he concentrated so hard on everything around him. He could imitate the call of every bird, and describe the idiosyncrasies of any animal from the track he left, whether the animal had to take a piss or wanted to make love. He could tell you how many limbs were in a tree, INSTANTLY, and tell you which limbs were preferred by the squirrels, birds, cats, or even ants. A long time ago, many, like this man, existed among our people. As you might be able to tell, there wasn't need for much talking when everybody knew most things. At this time I am talking about, however, he was the only one in the community like that.

His two friends loved to learn things from him but they could only master a skill in one thing, like the creation of efficacious traps or fletching arrows. They were mediocre in all else. You see, one had to concentrate very hard to know most things well, but there are hazards to knowing it all, as you shall see.

One day, his face fell off. He washed it in a creek. Some say it was cut off, stolen and sold. Poor, pitiful man, he couldn't even cry. What's to be done with him? He couldn't even

41

tell us what happened, or really happened. We were all curious. He simply went down to the creek to wash his face. He came back faceless, without a face. It just wasn't there.

Although this man was well informed and followed every rule, he did make a mistake. At that time, the custom required a person to offer tobacco as a gift to the water before one will wash their face. Otherwise, the Under Water Panther, will steal it, the face that is, and never will it be returned; although the man will live, he will live without a face. He probably was caught up in counting the scales of a sun fish and forgot to make his offering. Nobody really knows. You can see that this mistake can have drastic consequences, but it is not altogether without solutions. You see, this man had these two friends who were determined to help him.

This faceless man returned to our village following the knowledge still left in his feet and stood by the council fire while all the curious slowly mingled around:

"What's to be done with him?"

"He can't do much without a face."

"How will he eat?"

"How will he make himself useful?"

About everything was said but I don't think he could hear. You see, he didn't have ears. He just stood there: long black tangled hair, and long blank stare. Even his shadow lacked a face. He had a clear hole—bright as the ground underneath—where the sun passed through.

People were beginning to get worried.

"What's to be done with him," everybody said.

"Let's kill him. We can't have somebody with no face around here," said another.

Then:

"I will make him a face," cried out one friend.

"I will make him a face," shouted the other.

(By this time grandson, you will probably notice a familiar pattern. The university probably tells a similar story so you should anticipate what's coming.)

The council decided that making this man a new face was a good idea, even if making faces wasn't a practice of our people. We decided to give it a try anyway. The two friends left in different directions. We tied the faceless man to a post like a prisoner to keep him out of trouble, anticipating their return.

One friend examined ten thousand trees looking for the oldest, wisest, grandfather tree. He wanted to make a face out of wood but because his friend was so knowledgeable, he had to find a tree that had been around for a while, that had fought the wind for years, that had endured animals, insects, fire, cold, rains, and just about knew everything a tree could know. This was a hard task for this friend because he didn't know much about trees. He knocked on some, took the bark off others and looked underneath the bark of a lot more; he examined the leaves of several and even tasted the sap of a hundred more. Finally, he found one he liked: a tall black solemn tree showing the scars from constant battle with wind. Communities of moss, regiments of ants, it really is quite amazing, the abundance of life that exists on trees.

The carving was smooth and gentle: a surgical sawing. This friend took part of that tree and formed it into a distorted, deranged likeness of his face. It had large eyebrows, gigantic crooked nose, and elongated ears, with lips turned inside out, revealing a distorted whimsical smile. Tree wasn't hurt at all; the living piece of itself was so small that it wouldn't even be considered a scratch in man's terms.

Meanwhile, the other friend chose clay, but like the other, he wanted some clay with style—not some ordinary mud. And like the other, he didn't know much about what he was doing. He went all over digging and digging. He tried the mud underneath rivers but it simply washed away before he could get some. He tried making his own but ended up only making mud cakes. He dug in forests, out in clearings, by lakes, on top of hills, on the side of hills, under some moss, and in a hundred dried up river beds. He still couldn't find what he wanted. Most of the clay was too commonplace. Discouraged, he sat leaning against a tree thinking that he would never return to our village with an empty face.

Just then, he began watching the flight of some wasps. They landed in yellow mud. They appeared to be building nests out of this mud and some dead insects they had previously gathered. Delighted, he decided to make his clay out of these nests because of the diversity of things it was composed of: mud, wasp eggs, insect larvae, and a host of other things. He made a round face, with round eyes, and tiny round mouth, and small ears. He fired it for four days. When it was done, he hurried happily back home.

(Now, grandson, you will not be shocked at what will happen next. I think you have a pretty good idea that this story is bit ordinary for your tastes. You will just have to accept these commonplace themes.)

The two friends arrived on the same day. We sure were glad to see them because they were gone for a long time. Their friend was almost dead from starvation. He was no wider than the post we had tied him to. We also realized that now we had two faces. We didn't think to send these friends out together to make just one. Now we had two and we didn't know how to face this situation. Two faces, but which one? Now the wooden face had delicate features and would blossom in the spring but the clay face had a more worldly look and could take any form. Beauty? Versatility? The man had no say in the matter and we could not decide. The summer was almost over and soon everyone would disperse to hunt and gather supplies.

"That's it," said one. "With a wooden face in the forest, he could fool the deer and become a great hunter supplying our needs for years to come. He would have tree sense, the deer wouldn't mind him and he could ambush them easily, as well as other beasts, too."

"But, on the plain, or by beaver lodges, with his clay face, he could fool the buffalo, the otter and the beaver. Perhaps he could fool fish as well if he lay face up on the bottom of a lake or river. The fish would think him part of the bottom, part of the shoreline, or part of a bank," explained another.

This man was sure getting bothersome. Nobody could decide. "Let's kill him," said the one who said this before; "this man is too much trouble." We all wished he never lost his face. We went back to the creek to see if we could find it but when we looked in the water all we could see was ours. Now something had to be done. So we went searching for an answer and we ran across Nanabush picking some insects off a tree stump and eating them. "Hey, Nanabush, we will provide you with something better to eat if you can help us decide what's to be done with these two faces and this poor man."

We gave Nanabush most of our dried meat, half of our stored corn, berries, roots and things. We also gave him some tanned hides, black ash baskets, and a gigantic black kettle. You see, we didn't want to kill this man because we liked these two faces. We were willing to sacrifice all else to arrive at a solution. We waited for four weeks for Nanabush to decide. We also prepared for a long hard winter with less food than usual. We were sad at this prospect but eager to find out what Nanabush had to say about this matter.

He said: "The easy way was to kill this man, but after spending so much time trying to save him, I will help you. I will weave both faces onto his head. Therefore, all of you will be satisfied. I only hope you all think it was worth all the trouble and all the summer and all the fall, for now it is the beginning of winter."

When it was done, He–Who–Has–Two–Faces was the happiest man alive. He went out singing and dancing and he married two wives. He also ate up most of the remaining food. After the celebration, however, he helped everyone survive the winter. He was an amazing hunter and an enduring traveler. For he had to wander far and wide to procure food and then deliver it to the family most in need. He was a lot of help but by spring most realized that He–Who–Has–Two–Faces was very indecisive. Never could he make up his mind. You can imagine the indecision, wanting shade and wanting sun, sleeping indoors and sleeping outdoors. He traveled half the year and he stayed put for the other half. He became our greatest diplomat, traveling far into the forest, desert, and coast and all people seemed to like him. In the springtime, he was the most beautiful man that was ever seen with blossoms and green leaves growing madly across his head, out of his eyes, and under his tongue.

He spent half of his time outside our village and half of his time within. He could function in both the outside and the inner. He wasn't by any means dull anymore, nor was he all that knowledgeable about things. In a way, he was rather rude, forgetting half of our traditions, ceremonies, songs, and such. Even half our world refused to have any thing to do with him anymore. He had a two tracked mind and there was nothing we could do about it. After all, it was our fault. Although he could stand between our differences and look both ways, he was a bit of a nuisance. He persuaded half of our young to go hither toward there and hither toward here, learning things not very useful to our world. Half the time, he was a bad influence but he still remembered many useful things.

And he ended. *I adjusted the time-frame of the story to fit my own needs, and I probably told the story in a way that I would tell it. Unfortunately, I forgot all the names he used and most of the facts, so this story is only half accurate—no pun intended. At any rate, I created what I had to and I remembered the rest.*

OTHER POEMS

RIFLE AND WOMAN

Blue Woman laughing
at man and broken rifle

"fix that thing"
slipped in the creek

sophisticated bore
"you have broken muzzle"

Blue Woman friend
laugh, laugh, laugh

Rain–In–the–Face Talks to the Agency's Psychiatrist

Red Lake Singer beats the blue drum
Sings:

Bring forth the new
Please
I can't find out

Source,
Find it
Find it

I opened up
Expressed my toe as a crushed oak leaf
Stepped on — hear the source

Kicked a stone
The ripples went inward
And disappeared

Within the Lake.

BLACK ARROW (MANGLED INTENT)

From a forest an arrow shot.
Through a forest a road cut deep.

People move through the forest,
When the arrow propelled through strangeness

                           penetrated blackness
of a forest floor.

From the forest a people move,
Following the arteries of a wrinkled woman's hand.
Like blood they move,
                    transporting corn
                    dragging brown carved poles;
                    they stank
of animal flesh.

Only from the forest could the people move.
Strange, this old wrinkled woman's hand.
The people are her blood.
Then the forest is skin.

Then, the arrow penetrated black skin of a strange hand.
A self inflicted wound?
Logically,
The road is a capillary (an insignificant spillage of blood).

Sliced by the arrow,
The people spilled out.
The forest was a scene of
A dramatic amputation.

Yellow brown liquid spewed
Through warm flesh of a severed black hand.
The source of the arrow
Is believed to be from the other hand.

Brown corn liquid
Absorbing into pores forest floor
Dead flesh flaking off
The tepid smell of coagulated blood
The black wrinkles revealing a stark paleness

Through the deep cut road,
A people move.
The forest road clutching a stained

Black Arrow.

BLACK KETTLE

He psyched himself out
He poured white paints over himself
charged with a red hot
bloody rag flapping in air
space above his head
extended on a serpent carved stick
sweaty hands gripping

Red and White
Stripes—being dipped into
fired kettle
filled with buffalo
Stew

He has eyes
no nose
ears
or mouth
yet a tongue
straw bent slithers out
eyes catching flies in
sticky blood

He is blind
has scorched his tongue
rotting vegetables, carcass of horse

fallen, beside him
pinning his leg

His head cut
blood blinding eyes
in a corn field
mud stuck in ears

saber cut
nose

He has eyes
but cannot smell
eating insects
stuck to his blood — horse
sinking in mud

He contemplates
cutting off his leg, woe
the plowed corn
stuck in a furrow

His face bloody
like the flag beside
him

Ripped,
Shredded
— Hot red rag —
He feels himself
drag it
wave it.

CONTRARY MAN

He saw another self
Inside a frozen lily pond
A funny self
      —always doing things backwards—
Saying no when he means yes
Generally, just goofing around

At night, he slept
Early so as
To dream
About
His contrary self

He walked backwards
Among his people
Contrary Man

People don't mind him
They think him
Humorous
They like (and want)
One of these guys around

Little kids follow him
Around,
Teasing
Taunting him

He teased them back
Showing respect

An unchanging
Attitude he had for children

The problem with
Contrary Man is
He always thinks of himself
He gets engrossed
Playing his role

He likes that self
He saw him
In the frozen lily pond
He just couldn't
Get him

Off his mind

He began sleeping in day
Eating breakfast in
Evening

And when the people asked if he was to be
contrary
For a long time,
He said,
"No"

To have a Contrary Man
Around
          —does get kind of irritating—
These people were sure getting mad

The entertaining contrary
Becomes a nuisance

When he Beats his work song at night
When he shits in the Middle of camp

They had to do something about this!

So they took a huge cast iron kettle
Boiled some meat

Boiling hot,
They ask Contrary Man
To look at his self in
The meaty water

Then,
He reached with his arm through his
Reflection and grabbed
Some meat

He ate it
And became himself
And the people were not mad
anymore

This is what you should do
If Contrary Man happens to
Come
Among your people

You ask him
      —to eat up his old self—
So that he might become
Wholesome again
But, only after he goofs off for awhile

Six Killer Dies

Loading shells, made of sulfur
black powder — drinking whiskey
Two guns and cards

Fired red propellant
No white, greasy smoke
puffs of red,
red stone smoke

Six Killer shoots
him, twice, through each shoulder
cut and dried
prairie sheriff

Ch
>   *Er*
>   *O*
>   *Kee Lawman*

He ate cow — Texas fever longhorns —
He got himself a black mount, shelf clothes, and
silver badge/ He double loads all his guns.
He drinks expensive whiskey

His face looks like side of mountain
blue, chipped and vertical
He rides long and hard
Hunting children and taking them to cow farm
Methodist boarding school

Deuce of clubs, remember one-eyed king wild,
the diamond man and one other ace

give me two/ he gets three of diamonds,
two of hearts

He burned down the six,
orange, he burned down
red and black tripps—vertical
nose dropped down—chipped with red
stone—a crumpled bull on prairie green
cut and cut

the cards
are yellow
as the hands
with two guns

No white smoke
Feeling with face the green rug
Rising as he wonders about the tripps
the last whiskey drink
the red stone bull, dragged home, cow, he
crumpled like a half moon in his chair,
slouching down

He raised his hand to eat and the barrel of the
gun hit his chin, the edge
He stayed right there, pocketing his
badge

And ate his meat

WATER CARRIER

He enters fast
as fast as
he leaves
forgetting nothing

Giving water
he recedes
back

to ditches
to holes
to untapped water

fast as a gopher
as a snake
in and out of familiar
holes, crags, canyons

or even as a worm
diligent,
willing to be cut to pieces
to survive to enter fast

to plow
to cultivate
pierced by hooks
eaten by fish

Remembering
because
he was told to
remember

Gophers
with their heads
eaten by
buzzards
or shot off by
perfecting
cattle ranchers

Garden snakes
squirming
in wrinkled hands
seeking the touch of something
new, unfamiliar, strange, or exotic

Earth worms
pieces of flesh
continually
digging
pushing into
Earth, repeatedly

Especially
water holes,
found deep,

energy
uneaten flesh
providing

water

He will deliver
remembering flesh
an unending thirst

He carries buckets
to be filled
to be emptied and
filled

again and again
unpleasantly
he carries
not really wanting

replenishing
desiring
to stay

within
inside
earth flesh
like an earth worm
preferring to stay
in earth
but

surfaced by rain water

like snakes baking in sun

or gophers peeking out of holes

back and forth
bringing water
wanting to stay longer
he is forced out

drained of water, dehydrated
He is entering and leaving
continually

faster
he works
faster
he arrives

yet faster
he leaves
plunging down

like gopher
like snake
like worm

Working
forgetting nothing
always carrying water
always digging at earth

63

always coming to surface
then, going to find pure

unending water

finding dirt
dead gophers, uncomfortable snakes

worms

TITLE: THE EMPTY COLON

She: Open the door
      Count to five
      Enjoy your soup

He: Momma please be
      With me without
      Your pink dress

Narrator: The door opened
            Closed
            Opened
            Five times

            The soup burned his
            Tongue as the pink
            Dress dropped slowly
            To the ground

Empty:

LOCKED OUT

I,
outside
the window
saw my cat
looking
at me
inside,

I'm
locked out

Sometimes
I wonder
if the white and green
paint
needs a new coat

only,
I would paint it
sand
or
some kind of brown

But now,
I only want
to get in,

me in my
deer skin coat
ice cream cone in hand,

that cat
in the living
room window,

his chocolate ears,
face, tail, and paws
the rest of him
vanilla

staring at me with
those blue eyes —

Fucking Siamese
open the door.

ATOP THAT MILK–CRATE SHELF

I caught you
looking at the
moon,
cat

Staring at that
white disc,
through glass,
reflecting
my image
—in one's teeth—
incarnadine, unman
scarecrow

Your eyes
brilliant
as two of the
SEVEN SISTERS

your dark
silhouette
looking up through
foliage
scattered on
milk–crate shelf
angled like a telescope

So poised
your ears
flat back
as if ready
for flight

I
a prone
image
in
glazed
embrasure

read history
red war paint
—grappling hooks–
atoms,
formless and blue

Cat
a merciless
devourer
of animal flesh
jumps at the red
icy image
toward his prey

Robin and Starling
who replace the
moon in
daylight

What a Lousy Day for Outdoor Work

Bury me in a pine box
with the chocolate and vanilla painted cat
with The Complete Sherlock Holmes
with Sky and Telescope
and my chess pieces

       I am a lonely man
       painting this back wall
       white and green

Bury me in a pine box
and get out of this house
and take the black dog
and the small car
with banged out head–lights

       I'm sequestered in
       back yard
       raking those brown
       orange leaves left over from
       last fall

Bury me in a pine box
with my white Ford pick–up truck
with a loaded Winchester model '64
with grandpa's World War One helmet
and an eagle feather

I ain't feeling so hot
agitating this gravel
in the driveway

Bury me in a pine box
and come home to bake bread
and to feed that old black dog
and that tired old cat
with eyes only for you

I'm not so sure
I can care for those
flowers and bushes
left rudely unintended

On this lousy day for outdoor work

These Are Not Haiku

down in the well
looking for water
"for Christ's sake"

eating seafood in New Orleans
drinking Australian beer
"because it was there"

one hill off toward
right side of shoulder
reflecting light
of his rank

my bike
totally demolished
I
unhurt
went to a movie

the fish
flopped, died
of dehydration
the salty deck

wet and salty cards
cracked
I
won fifty bucks

kitty cat
hey you cat
stop shitting
by the garbage

WHALE WATCHERS ON TOP OF NEWFOUNDLAND CLIFFS

I.

Whale watchers on top of Newfoundland cliffs, peering, seeking the great water spouts, the prize of their endeavors.

They stand straight up with hiking boots and Arctic parkas distorting their forms, binoculars strapped around their necks and refractor telescopes strategically placed—aiming downward at whales—resembling the hated harpoon gun.

They stand, peering, straining to see these great mammals while clinging to black rock, their faces feeling the salt wind and tanning in the cold sun. Black sails interrupt their search.

Black smoke sails of whaling ship—enemy of the whale watchers. The seekers hate these ships that come close to hear whale songs.

At their distance, they only observe the surface breathing of these great beings, the great water spouts through binocular eyes, the rolling of oceanic waves.

What do whale watchers really know about whales? They stand aloft
peering down around noses at beings they never touch.

They make whale buttons, read whale books, raise whale flags and regurgitate their presumptuous whale–like feelings through popular press. They watch Jacques Cousteau and study high powered photos of whale babies.

These watchers do not believe Herman Melville. They
see the great white devil in the gray–black steel of
whaling vessel.

Strange to see ships that resemble whales, the gun powder
harpoons, the Moby Dick of steel: "Sink the Pequot, sink
the Pequot," yell whale hunters with Japanese and
Russian tongues.

What do these whale hunters really know about whales?
They kill them and squeeze their flesh like sponges filled
with exotic waters. They see no mind or beauty—object,
object of their endeavors.

II.

I watched
a whale once,
landlocked
in a tiny inlet cove

one night,
when a raging storm
produced
50 foot waves,
whale, pursuing his feed

slipped over
jagged black rocks,
unknowingly

In the morning,
townspeople
shot it to death in
target practice frenzy

as the town biologist
flew down to Mexico
to study the behavior of whales from
century old whale bones

His mate waited
outside, in the relative
freedom of ocean, for
his return

She died of starvation as the
townspeople towed
her mate
out to sea,

when his decomposing
body contaminated
their drinking
water

Oh, whale
Oh, whale

I wished I
could have
talked to
you

THE KID

He cried.
He knowing why the tree-house was
being torn down.
Rebuilt, backlawn
hammered back together underneath
the big oak,

That big tree,
with limbs sawed off,
next to the buried milkman's box

That received little boy's secrets,
toys and mice and pigtails and
chess
pieces, rocks and flowers and dead
spiders,

Not simply Ashley Dairy's
pint-sized glass bottles filled
with white milk.

He hated milk.
He liked the tree-house and
the buried milkman's box.

Both held secrets and fun.
But, both were different.
The milkman's box only he knew
about.

But, the tree-house he didn't even
build.

And when
he rolled out of the tree-house
When ten feet off the ground,
He could still hear his mother cry,
"Now goddammit didn't
I tell you somebody was
going to get hurt."

He did cry (a little)
But he knew fun,
To jump and pounce, to roll around,
Even with a split open head with
blood gushing out.

He cried.
Really, when they ripped the nails
out of the branches and the boards
came crashing down.
Now the tree-house would not be so
much fun
rebuilt back on the ground.

He still had the milkman's box,
That little aluminum box that could
hold four whole pints of milk.

He did steal it
From the front porch.
He did not know that;
He sought fun.

Anyway, the dairy replaced it with
another

And
He only wanted one,
To be buried with little red
shovel,
To hold only his secrets:

Dad's favorite pipe, mom's
necessary hair spray,
Brother's favorite Tonka truck,
older brother's cigarettes and
Sister's love letters — especially
sister's love letters.
She was furious — he was only having
fun —

But the tree-house he liked too.
He was disappointed that
it had to come down.
But it was going to be rebuilt
right next to the milkman's box.

Would they find it?
He hoped not.
It was too much fun.

The tree-house on the ground!
What would he call it?
A ground-house?
No this would not do.

He cried,
For the tree-house to be
put back up in the tree.
After all,
that was where it belonged.

Nothing doing—"We can't have
little boys falling out of tree-
houses
No more
—No sir ree—"

He was mad.
He stopped crying.
No sir ree   —aye—

"Well,
I'll teach 'em."

So, he began to hide more things:

Mom's new wig, dad's automotive timing
light, brother's Mickey
Mouse watch,
Older brother's tennis shoes,
and sister's diaphragm
—especially sister's Diaphragm—

She was walking around like the
wicked witch of the north;
He was only having fun; after all, he
didn't know what it was.

The milkman's box was getting
pretty full and
the lid was sticking out of the
ground.
The whole family was in an uproar,
wondering where all their things
were.

He did not mind.
He only asked if the tree-house
would be put back up in the tree.

He pleaded his case before
they got it totally rebuilt
back on the ground.

No sir ree!

But then his dad noticed the lid:

"What's my timing light doing in
here and there's little brother's
Tonka truck And his watch — My
PIPE! — and mom's wig — and what's
this hair spray doing in here, and
older brother's shoes, and all of
this paper. What in the heck is
this? Hey, darling!
Come over here."

You can imagine the uproar,
The screaming and yelling.
He did not understand.

He cried.
He only wanted the tree-house
back up in the tree.
What was wrong with that?

A long time would pass before
he would have any fun —
I guess that was the only thing
he was sad about.

No more tree-house!
Only a ground-house!
And of course,
no more milkman's box.

Oh, he did admit everything.
After all, he was only having fun.

Sweet Grass and Sun

Burn sweet grass
rinse your face
with smoke

Eat the moon
slowly, then spit
the pieces out

Eat it again
spit it out

Burn sweet grass
wash your hands
with smoke

Speak the wind
angrily, then cover
sky with hand

Speak again
cover sky dark

Burn sweet grass
bath your body
smoke, smoke

Lick the earth
sun, don't let
it melt

Smoldering sweet grass
cleanse my face
with smoke